HOW TO GET THROUGH COLLEGE

AND WHAT I WISH SOMEONE TOLD ME

HOW TO GET THROUGH COLLEGE

AND WHAT I WISH SOMEONE TOLD ME

An easy-to-follow guide with advice on how to navigate through college, what to expect, and how to make good decisions

FIRST EDITION

ALEXIS WILLIAMS

Copyright © 2020 Alexis Williams

This is a work of non-fiction.

All rights reserved. No part of this book may be reproduced or transmitted in any form or by any means, electronic storage, and retrieval system, except in the case of brief quotations embodied in critical articles or reviews, without permission in writing from the publisher.

In no way is it legal to reproduce, duplicate, or transmit any part of this document in either electronic means or in printed format. Recording of this publication is strictly prohibited and any storage of this document is not allowed unless with written permission from the publisher. All rights reserved.

ISBN NO. 978-1-943409-88-4

Printed in the United States of America

THIS BOOK IS DEDICATED TO

- High school students
- College students
- Anyone intending to attend college
- Anyone going back to college
- Parents
- Educators

- My nephew's, neice and god children

And to anyone in need of motivation in navigating through the challenges of college.

This is for you.

Table of Contents

Introduction 1

Activity 3

Chapter 1: Alexis Williams 11

*What I Wish Someone
Told Me About Adjusting To A New School* 13

Chapter 2: High School 17

*What I Wish Someone
Told Me About High School* 20

Chapter 3: Choosing The Right College 23

*What I Wish I Knew
About Choosing The Right College* 24

Chapter 4: The Start Line 29

*What I Wish Someone
Told Me About The Start Line* 33

Chapter 5: Dorm Life! 39

*What I Wish Someone
Told Me About Dorm Life* 43

Chapter 6: When Financial Aid Hits 47

*What I Wish Someone
Told Me About When Financial Aid Hits* 49

Chapter 7: Peer Pressure 53

   What I Wish Someone
   Would Have Told Me About Peer Pressure 55

Chapter 8: Tutoring, And Office Hours................................ 59

   Reach Out For Help 60

   What I Wished Someone
   Would Have Told Me About
   Tutoring And Office Hours 61

Chapter 9: Get Involved With Your Campus!........................ 65

   What I Wish Someone
   Told Me About Getting Involved With Campus 67

Chapter 10: Life Got In The Way.. 71

   What I Wish Someone
   Told YOU About Life Getting In Your Way..................... 71

Chapter 11: Is College For Me? 77

   Activity 77

Chapter 12: The Finish Line.. 83

   What I Wish Someone
   Told YOU About The Finish Line 84

   Self-Care Activity 90

GRADUATION 93

   What Does It Mean
   To Be A Black Graduate Today? 95

About Author... 103

Special Thanks to

My mother, Juanita Banks, for always, providing, nurturing, believing, and being present in all my important life changes and accomplishments, I would not be the woman I am today without you.

Some of my family members such as Steven Williams, Kenisha Hodnett, Tywon White, Pamela Banks, Michael Springfield, Keymoney Dawson, Diana Banks, and Harper, for motivating me to pursue my dreams and being there for me, I am truly grateful for each one of you.

My friends Ver'Na Rogers, Danise Webb, Yadira Soto-Robledo, Markasia Broadnax, and Kendon Tillis, for listening, encouraging, challenging, speaking confidence in me, and believing in me. Each one of you helped me reach my full potential in completing this book.

Introduction

This book is a product of experiences that I encountered while navigating through the challenges of college with little to no guidance from anyone. This book is intended to motivate, encourage, and inspire anyone intending to go back to college, or begin college. It also holds the purpose to ensure current college students graduate college, high school students attend college, empower individuals to follow their dreams and pursue finding their purpose, drive, and vision.

Activity

Before you begin reading this book, I would like for you to complete an activity. In this activity, you will write down 10 long-term or short-term goals that you would like to accomplish within the next five years.

Directions

Write 10 long term or short-term goals that you would like to accomplish within the next five years down here:

1.) _____

2.) _____

3.) _____

4.) _____

5.) _____

6.) _____

7.) _____

8.) _____

9.) _____

10.) _____

Now that you are finished writing down your goals, answer the following questions:

- What are the steps needed to achieve each goal?

  _____

  _____

  _____

  _____

  _____

- Are your goals realistic?

  _____

  _____

  _____

  _____

  _____

How to Get Through College
And What I Wish Someone Told Me

- Who can help you achieve these goals?

  _____
  _____
  _____
  _____
  _____

- How long will it take you to accomplish each goal?

  _____
  _____
  _____
  _____
  _____

- What will you do to remain on task to complete each goal?

  _____
  _____
  _____
  _____
  _____

Take Away:

Goals are important to have because they will keep you motivated, focused, committed, accountable, and inspired. Remember to always stick to your goals and never let anyone steer you away from pursuing your goals.

66

All it takes is a simple
thought of
pursuing something.

- Alexis Williams

Statistics

Statistics show that 30% of college freshmen drop out after their first year of college. "Conflict between school, job, and family. Most individuals find it difficult to tend to their loved ones, work, and attend college at the same time. "

Atlas, College. U.S College Dropout Rate and Dropout Statistics. August 12th, 2014. https://www.collegeatlas.org/college-dropout.html#:~:text=30%25%20of%20college%20freshmen%20drop,for%20dropping%20out%20of%20college.

- Lack of motivation, inspiration, and confidence.
- Most importantly, the financial struggle.

> Statistics suggest that I was not going to succeed, that I was either going to drop out of school or work a minimum wage job for the rest of my life, but I REFUSE to be another statistic!
>
> **- Alexis Williams**

CHAPTER 1

ALEXIS WILLIAMS

I was raised in a single-parent household in various locations of Los Angeles, California. I attended Henry Clay middle school located in Los Angeles, California for my 7th grade middle school year. While attending Henry Clay middle school, I began following my friend's bad choices instead of being a leader. My mother began to pick up on my behaviors when I started hiding my report cards, ditching classes, and receiving bad grades. One day, I was at school and I was scheduled to be in math class, but there I was, hanging out on the P.E field with my friends. I hated being in math class! I hated math! While on the P.E Field, a staff member on the intercom stated, "Will Alexis Williams please report to the main office, I repeat, will Alexis Williams please report to the main office."

I thought, *well, there could be someone else at this school with the same name as mine*, I then quickly realized that the announcement probably was for me, being that I was ditching class right then. I slowly walked to the office with sweaty hands and a racing heartbeat. I thought, *damn they go call my mamma then I am going to be on punishment!*

I walked into the office and saw my mother sitting in the chair.

She then asked, "Why aren't you in your math class?"

I responded, "I was, I just went to the P.E field after I used the bathroom to see my friends. (She knew I was lying my ass off). What are you doing here?"

She responded, "I was coming to you check you out of school early to go get food and spend time with you."

We then left the school, got something to eat, and hung out with each other.

The next morning, I got dressed for school and I thought that everything was okay because my mother never said that I was grounded or in any trouble. I then asked my mother if she could take me to school. She replied, "You're not going back to that school anymore, you're going to be bussed to the valley for the new school year that is coming up you will be attending Portola Middle School."

I only had another two to three weeks to finish out my 7th-grade year at Henry Clay Middle School.

I began to cry and said, "All of my friends are at Henry Clay and I don't want to change schools. I promise I won't skip class again, I promise!"

My mother responded, "You'll find new friends."

When the fall semester of my 8th-grade year came, I was on a school bus to the valley. I was so nervous and so shy, I did not know how far the school was from my house, nor did I have a class schedule. My first day was the worse day ever! I did not have any classes, nor did I know where any classes were located, so I asked my peers for directions around the campus. I remember getting home from school on the first day, begging my mother to let me go back to Henry Clay middle school. I told my mother that I did not believe that I was smart enough to attend Portola Middle School because the classes seemed harder than Henry Clay's Middle School classes. She did not budge. I then had to suck it up and continue attending Portola Middle School. Ironically, I ended up loving Portola Middle School! I met lifelong friends and received a better education. After graduating from Portola Middle School, I attended Reseda High School that was also located in the Valley for the full four years of high school.

What I Wish Someone Told Me About Adjusting To A New School

- I wish that someone would have told me that I am just as smart as my peers.
- Things that are new, are only new temporarily.
- You will meet new friends.

- You will adapt to your new environment.
- Anything is possible if you put your mind to it.
- Be a leader.

Take Away:

It is okay to be afraid of starting a new school. Remember that you can overcome all your fears and you will adapt to the new environment.

> It is natural to feel scared while starting a new journey, you will adapt as time progresses.

- Alexis Williams

CHAPTER 2

HIGH SCHOOL

My Experience

I attended Reseda Senior High School for the full four years of high school. High school was one of the most memorable experiences of my life! High school was "**LIT**!" There were games to attend almost every Friday, school dances, field trips, prom, and so much more! High school was where I began to see myself grow physically and mentally.

I became a cheerleader during my senior year of high school. To remain on the team, I had to maintain a 2.0 grade point average or above, and I could not miss any days of school because I had practice and games most days after school. Although I was a part of the cheerleading team, my grades in high school were not so good. I was barely holding my head above water by doing the bare minimum which was attending class and passing each test with a C or better. My mindset in high school was to pass each test with a C because technically a C was a passing grade and that was all I cared about. Sadly, I tended to do the bare minimum in high school. I used to think that if I got all Cs, then I would be good. Shit, even a D was passing. My mindset was that no one in my household finished high school, so why should I go above and beyond if graduating high school wasn't all that matters? I did not have anyone to motivate me to get better grades and stay on track.

When I was a senior in high school, I met with my school counselor about attending college. She told me that I would have to attend a community college because my overall grade point average would not be acceptable to attend a university college. I remember not fully understanding what she meant by that. I thought, *welp college is college, community college here I come*. Over the next couple of days, I began to research the difference between attending a community college and a university. The biggest difference that caught my eye was living in the dorms. If I attended a community college I could not live on campus and lord knows I wanted to move out of my mother's house and be on my own.

I did not know exactly what I wanted to do after graduating high school, I just knew that I wanted to move out of my mother's home, work with children as a teacher, social worker, or working at a day-care center.

Towards the end of my senior year of high school, my grade point average was 1.95. I needed at least a 2.0 to get accepted into any university (which I was told by my counselor). I shared with my counselor that I would prefer to attend a university instead of a community college and if there was anything else that could be done. I then asked my counselor if it was possible to take additional classes to boost my grade point average My counselor responded no. My counselor then informed me that there is a program available at some college universities called the Educational Opportunity Program, which gives prospective students who have a low grade point average an opportunity to still attend college under the condition that you attend summer school. I became extremely excited about attending college because of this! I then started to think about what kind of job I was going to get if I only had a high school diploma. I've heard people say, "You'll be working at McDonald's or Walmart with only a high school diploma." Though there is absolutely nothing wrong with working at McDonald's or Walmart, I wanted more for myself.

I also found out that I could live on campus! I started to get even more excited! I began googling the nearest university campuses near me. Although I wanted to move out of my mother's house, I was still a mamma's girl and I needed her close to me. I told my mother how excited I was to attend college. My mother then stated, "I cannot afford to send you to college."

I responded, "My counselor said that I can apply for financial aid!" I then began applying to university colleges.

What I Wish Someone Told Me About High School

- I was not aware that my grades in my junior and senior years of high school mattered the most if I wanted to get accepted into a university college. Trust me, if I had known that, I wouldn't have joined the cheerleading team during my freshman year of high school for motivation in keeping me on track! I never challenged myself to go above and beyond.

- Have you ever heard someone say, "Stay ready so you don't have to get ready." The moment you are in the 9th grade you should be striving to achieve the highest grades possible. That means studying every day, asking questions in class when you are not understanding something, attending tutoring after school, joining a sport, etc. You have to stay in this mindset of doing the best that you can so when you are a junior and a senior and you begin to have discussions about college, GPA, SAT scores, etc., you will be ready without trying to do extra credit assignments to bring your grades up. Once you master this mindset, you will give your all in anything that you do throughout your life.

- You can take college courses for your freshman year while you are attending high school! For free! Cool right!?

- Taking college courses while you are in high school will keep you motivated to attend college AND taking a college course before attending college will help you finish college faster! I know that this will be additional work and determination, but this will save you time and jump start your college journey. When you earn college credit you don't have to take as many courses when you start college.

- Please check out the 2020 Modern States Education Alliance. https://modernstates.org/freshman-year-free/

Take Away:

Think about your future! Look into the website above to see what they have to offer. Be sure to maintain good grades throughout your high school journey.

> Always give 100%
> in anything that you do
> so you won't ever have to
> wonder what if.
>
> - Alexis Williams

CHAPTER 3

Choosing the Right College

Choosing the right college can be an overwhelming decision. There are so many factors to consider, such as distance, cost, family, friends and so much more! Choosing a college to attend is one of the first major adult decisions that you will make for yourself. You must weigh your options. There are numerous different colleges such as community colleges, university of California colleges, private colleges, California state universities, historical black colleges, and so many more!

My Experience

While in high school, I applied to California State University Northridge, California State University Dominquez Hills, and California State University Los

Angeles and the educational opportunity program at each school. I really wanted to go to California State University Northridge because if you attended Reseda High School, the closest college would be Northridge University, and most of my friends from Reseda High School were applying to Northridge University.

I did not apply to any community colleges because I had my mind set on attending a university college. I wanted to see if I was going to be accepted into any universities before I applied to a community college. ***Granted there is not anything wrong with attending a community college.*** However, I wanted to live on campus to experience college in its entirety.

I decided that I wanted to stay in California to attend college. I was too afraid to leave home and my mother did not want me to move far away. My mother's opinion weighed heavily on my decision making. I did not have anyone to go to for direction as to which college to choose and the difference between the colleges I applied to. I had to research the college campuses on my own, knowing that I did not know what I was specifically looking for.

What I Wish I Knew About Choosing The Right College

- One of the first things to consider when choosing a college is if you would like to stay closer to home or if you would like to move far away from home. Some of the pros with attending college near your home is having the opportunity to stay home and attend college or move into your own apartment or a dorm and still have the leisure to go back home to visit your family and friends. Some of the cons with moving far away from home are that you will not be able to see your family and friends as much as you might desire and you will also have to find new friends and adapt to a new environment.

- You must consider what you are going to major in. Some campuses have better major programs than others. For Example, if you wanted to major in nursing, you should research the top colleges for nursing programs, the same goes for any other major. It is also okay to have an undecided major because you will start off with taking general education classes which will give you time to choose a major. But don't take too much time! **YOU DO NOT WANT TO WASTE TIME AND MONEY ON NOT CHOOSING A MAJOR.**

- You should take into consideration the pricing of each campus you are considering. Are you attending college on a full-ride scholarship? Are your parents/family paying for you to attend college? Will you work and pay for college yourself? Or will you apply for grants and loans?

- Let's not forget about living arrangements! If you attend a community college, you will NOT have the opportunity to reside on campus as community colleges do not have that option. Are you tired of living with your parents or whomever you are residing with and want to move out? Then attending a university may be a better fit for you as you will be allowed to reside on campus. If you decide to attend a community college, you will be able to transfer to a four-year university after you meet transfer requirements which usually takes two years.

- If you decide to go straight to a university college, you will have the benefit of living on campus. Living in the dorms provides you with independence and the opportunity to grow independently and make your own decisions!

- Visiting prospective colleges is also a good idea. Seeing and walking through a prospective college versus seeing pictures online is always better, it is better than looking through the lens of others. Many colleges offer tours that you can take. Although, this may not be possible if you are thinking of attending a college that is out of state due to not being able to financial issues, you can contact staff via phone and ask for a virtual overview of their campus. Don't be afraid to seek help and ask questions!

- As there are a number of things to consider, try to be open-minded about your options. You can also make a list of the good and bad that may come out of choosing a college. After you weigh your options. **DON'T PROCRASTINATE!** You will have to make your decision on which college you are going to attend before the deadline that they give you.
- You CAN afford to attend college.

Take away

Regardless of which route you take, remember that this is the time where you should make decisions based on what **YOU** want not what anyone else wants for you.

> On a mission, your worse enemy is idle time.

— Nipsey Hustle (Rest in Peace)

CHAPTER 4

The Start Line

Your first year of college is going to be one of the **BEST** years of your college journey. This will also be the year where you are going to be truly tested mentally and physically. You are going to make **A LOT** of new friends and attend parties almost every day. NO CAP!

My Experience

The day before my 18th birthday, I checked the mail and guess what! I had gotten conditionally accepted into California State University Los Angeles through the Educational Opportunity Program!!! This was a bittersweet moment for me because I really wanted to attend California State University Northridge, but overall, I was extremely excited. I remember having my 18th birthday party at a bowling alley and announcing to my friends and family that I would be attending California State University in the fall of 2011. No one in my family had gone to college and I wanted to set a new tone. And there I was, a first-generation college student in my family.

I began attending California State University Los Angeles in June of 2011, because I was accepted conditionally, I had to attend the summer bridge program. I took four classes during summer bridge which were P.E, English, Math, and Pan Africa Studies which the campus paid for. Because the Educational Opportunity Program accepted me into the school conditionally, I had to pass each class with a C or better and if I did not pass each class with a C or better, I would not be accepted into California State University Los Angeles in the fall semester. Crazy right? It was like a preliminary round.

When I sat in my first college classroom, I was beyond amazed! The classroom was huge and there were over 50 students in one classroom! I was not used to that. I was only used to being in smaller classroom settings. I liked sitting in the front or middle of the classroom because I am nearsighted and the majority of the time, I forgot to take my glasses to class with me.

I gave my ALL into passing each class. I never wanted something so bad in my life! At the end of the summer semester, I passed ALL the classes and I was OFFICIALLY a student at California State University Los Angeles.

For the fall semester of my freshman year, I had to take remedial math and English. I remember crying to my friends and family because I could not seem to pass the remedial math class. Like most of my peers, I wanted to give up on school. I kept thinking, if I cannot pass this remedial math class, how can I pass any of my upper-level math classes? What kept me going was being embarrassed to fail. I have always had the mindset of caring about what other people think of me, I wanted to prove to my friends and family that I can make it through this and graduate. I kept that momentum going throughout college.

One of my favorite things about college is that you created your own schedule! I was always a morning person because I used to have to wake up every morning at 5 am to get ready for school because my school bus left at 6:15 am. For the fall semester of my freshman year, I took mostly morning classes beginning at 8 am. Majority of the time I had between two to three classes per day, Monday through Thursday. Although some classes were offered on Fridays and Saturdays, most students I did not have classes on Fridays and rarely on Saturdays.

Another one of my favorite things about college was that I had classes with different races and ages! I loved seeing people from all around the world in my classes because it gave me additional confirmation that anyone of any race or age can attend college and nobody can tell you any different!

When I first started college, my major was child development. I just knew that I wanted to become a preschool teacher. I took one child development class during my freshman year and realized that I did not want to obtain a degree in child development because the class did not interest me. I then changed my major to Sociology after a year of being undecided.

My Experience In Choosing The Right Classes, Professors, And Schedule

Every semester I was given a registration date to register for my classes for the upcoming semester. A couple of days before my registration date I had to figure out which classes I wanted to take. My academic counselor provided me with a road map of all the classes I needed to take for my major in order to graduate college. This information was also available on my college website. I liked attending classes back to back without breaks in between. For example, if my first class was from 10 am-11:30 am, I would have another class from 12 pm-1:30 pm and so forth. The morning of registration always gave me anxiety. There were hundreds of students who were also registering for classes at the same time. The day before registration I put all of the classes I wanted to take in my cart in my online portal. I had to make sure I pressed submit the moment it was my time to register for classes. Sometimes I got lucky and got all of my classes that were in my cart, and other times I only got two out of four classes that were in my cart, therefore, I had to look for another class or a different time.

My academic counselor also informed me that I should maintain a balance in my schedule. If I were taking math, English, and history, I would add in an extracurricular activity class.

My peers informed me that there was a website called Rate My Professor (2020 Altice USA News, Inc. Rate My Professors, https://www.ratemyprofessors.com/) which allows students to assign ratings to professors based on the level of difficulty, if a textbook was needed, classroom structure, and so much more. I tended to visit ratemyprofessor.com almost every time I enrolled in a new class. Everyone has their own opinion about an individual that you may not agree with but ratemyprofessor.com gave me insight into how the class is going to be.

What I Wish Someone Told Me About The Start Line

- Go to college they said. It would be fun they said. That may be true and all, but did anyone ever tell you that college will be a struggle? No, right? You see college movies and you would think that college is all fun and play and you will possibly meet the love of your life. I'll be the first to tell you that that's not the reality for most individuals. College comes with a lot of hard work and dedication.

- Your group of friends may go from a circle of ten to fifteen individuals in the first year of college to about three or four individuals by junior year. Not because you and your friends had a falling out, but because their grades started to drop and they were on academic probation for a while.

- Do not be surprised if you are taking classes with people who are twice your age. Yes, I said TWICE YOUR AGE. That is the beauty of college! There is no age limit! You can attend school at whatever age you desire! As long as you can do, the work you can take the class.

- I will be the first to tell you that morning classes may not be the best idea if you are not a morning person! Granted, you will be done with your classes earlier in the day, but you are also risking not going to class because you are too tired to wake up. Most freshmen in college do not have a job during their very first semester, so if this is the case, do not be in a rush to go anywhere. Sleep in and start your classes between 9 am-10 am. If you are not a morning person at all, then you can take night classes! Most night classes begin at 6 pm so you will have the opportunity to sleep in and start your day later!

- Some of the first classes you are going to take within the first two years of college are your general ED classes which are math, English, history, etc.

Basically, the classes you just finished taking while you were in high school. (I know it did not make any sense to me neither.)

- It will take you approximately two years to complete your general ED classes if you are attending school full time. After you are done with your general Ed classes, you will begin taking the classes for your major and you are only going to go up from there. Once you begin taking your major classes, you will become more eager to finish college because your major classes are the most fun! I loved taking my Sociology classes because this was a subject that I was interested in.

- You will have the opportunity to double major, get a minor, a certificate, etc.

- Buy used books! I know most of you may not use Facebook anymore, but let me tell you! Cal State La book exchange page was lit! We bought and sold books on that page for the low and we met on campus which was a safe exchange. Look into what social media account your school offers so that you and your peers can exchange books. You will save a lot of money by buying used books versus new books. Plus, you will not need the book again after you are done with the class.

- Try not to take classes in the summer of freshman year unless you are repeating a class that you previously failed. Give yourself a break! I understand you want to graduate faster, but you also need a break to re-charge yourself. Too much of something can ultimately cause you to become burnt out. You will graduate at your own time and at your own pace.

- You might come across a lot of attractive people during college! Yes, I said it! We are human and temptation will present itself! Have fun, but not too much fun! When you become physically and emotionally attracted to someone, you tend to make poor decisions based on wants not needs.
- Never let anyone steer you away from your dreams and goals and if they do not understand that, then they are not the right person for you. Never allow anyone to manipulate your mind! Never allow anyone to walk over you and use you! And NEVER EVER complete anyone else's schoolwork for them!
- Do not take too many classes at once to graduate school quicker, taking too many classes at once will cause you to have more stress and anxiety than you already have with adjusting to being a college student. Take classes that are interesting to you as well. College is all about how many CREDITS you have. Of course, you have to take classes that are required in order for you to graduate but you can also throw in a dance class, art, yoga, etc., anything

fun that you would like to try. This way, you will have a class to look forward to going to.
- Rest! A good night's sleep is extremely important for effective work.

Take Away:

Take your time! Do not be in a rush to graduate! You are not on anyone's time but your own. Enjoy college!

> I believe that we all have a purpose. We MUST be willing to put in the work to find it.
>
> -Alexis Williams

CHAPTER 5

DORM LIFE!

My Experience

I was so excited to move out of my mother's home. No more asking for permission to go to places or to have company, no curfew? What! Yaaass!

I have always had my own room, so the thought of having to share a room with a stranger was a bit terrifying. I started to think about all the things that can go wrong with having a roommate such as, is she going to snore? Is she going to have a lot of guys over? Is she going to clean up after herself? Can I trust her alone with my belongings? What if she is crazy!? The list went on and on. Ultimately, I had to get over all my fears and go for it. I wanted to have the complete college experience and that for me meant living in the dorms.

The first day I moved in, I was nervous to meet my roommate. My mother took me to the market to buy food and snacks. She also helped me move my belongings inside my dorm room. When it was time for her to leave, I started crying. Why was I crying? My mother stayed 25 minutes away from Cal State LA and I could go back home to see her at any time. Plus, I wanted to leave my mother's house so bad because I was "grown" and there I was crying like a big ass baby. I cried because this was the first time I was going to be living on my own, cooking for myself, and having responsibilities.

The first night in the dorms was so LIT! There was a mixer in the quad area which consisted of the new freshman, it was a chance for us to get to know each other, and then there was an after-party at someone's dorm.

Having more freedom is great! There is no curfew, I did not have to tell my mom where I was going, who I was going to be with, and what time I was coming home because I did not live with her anymore. I was !iving my best life!

Freshman year, my dorm room consisted of two bedrooms and one bathroom. Two women to a room. There were other dorms that consisted of four bedrooms and two bathrooms which means that it was eight girls in total. Crazy right? Keep in mind that the dorms at every campus are different. Some dorms may have a single person in a room while others may have three people in a room. It varies, depending on the campus your attending. Luckily, I resided in a two-bedroom dorm with two individuals per room.

My first roommate was cool. She went home on the weekends, so from Thursday night to Sunday night, I had the room to myself. My roommates in the other room were also cool, we all had different schedules, so we were not always there at the same time.

There will be rules and regulations that you must follow while residing in the dorms. Rules such as no overnight guest, no parties, no loud music after a certain time, no pets, etc. Each campus is different and will have its own rules. I have been written up before, due to loud music coming out of my dorm from a kickback I was throwing. I also had my friends and my boyfriend spend the weekend at my dorm. I knew that these were things that I should not do but everyone else did, so I thought that I should too! Usually, there will be staff that resides in the dorms 24/7 for any emergencies and to keep an eye out for any parties or individuals who do not attend the university. The majority of the time, staff will not know who attends the school and who does not attend the school, so as long as your roommates are okay with you having company over, you will be fine. We are human, so there will be times where your friends will want to spend the night at your dorm, but do not do this to often. Try to abide by the rules and be respectful of others because if you get written up too many times, you can get kicked out of the dorm.

During the second semester of my freshman year, my roommate decided that she wanted to move back home, and I then got a new roommate. This new roommate was the opposite of my first roommate. She did not like to clean up after herself and she never went home on the weekends!

I remember, one day I woke up and there was a man lying in her bed with her wide awake. The night before, I went to bed with just a T-Shirt and underwear on and I had to use the restroom, but I was afraid to get out of my bed because I did not want him to see me. All I was thinking was, *who was this guy?* Why wouldn't she tell me that she was going to have company? I couldn't hold my pee any longer, I got up and ran to the restroom while holding my shirt down with my hands so that my butt was covered with my shirt. After walking out of the restroom, there was another male walking from the living room going into the restroom. I asked him who he was and he said he was a friend of the guy who was in the bed with my roommate!

As soon as her guest left, I told my roommate how I felt. I told her that it was okay for her to have company, but she should have warned me first. These are some of the uncomfortable conversations you are going to have to have with your roommates. Set boundaries and do not let people walk all over you. If I would have never told her how I felt, she would have never known, and she probably would have done it again.

I resided in the dorms for the first two years of college and then I moved back home. I moved back home because although dorm life was extremely fun, it was also expensive. I decided that the money I was receiving to live in the dorms could go into my own pocket. However, I am happy that I chose to reside in the dorms to get the full college experience.

What I Wish Someone Told Me About Dorm Life

- If you are thinking about living in the dorms, you should contact staff and inquire about the different kinds of rooms they have so that you can know what you are going to be facing.

- You are going to have uncomfortable conversations with your roommates. Set boundaries and do not let people walk all over you.

- You can have a complete college experience without living in the dorms as well! Some people prefer to stay at home to save money or simply because living in the dorms is not something that they would like to do. I had friends who did not stay on campus for their entire college journey and loved living at home. You should always make the decision on whatever it is that YOU want to do not what anyone else wants you to do. I say this because a lot of individuals' families would like for them to stay at home because they are not ready to let go, or because they depend on them to help financially.

- You may be living with people who you do not like for whatever reason. But remember that the only person you can control is yourself and know that you are there to complete school. You also should not feel like you are walking on eggshells, so if something is bothering you, let it be known. The worst thing you can do is let all the little things that your roommate does pile up and then explode. Speak out as you see things occurring.
- Mark your food! When you go grocery shopping, be sure to tell your roommates not to eat or drink anything that you bought unless you would like to share.
- Set boundaries, rules, and expectations with your roommates.
- Have monthly meetings with your roommates.
- Don't be afraid to speak up and stand up for yourself!

Take Away

There are many individuals who MUST live on campus because they are coming from a different state or do not have any family or friends who they can reside with. It might be an extremely hard transition because you may not know anyone, the neighborhoods, food, and culture may be unfamiliar to you, but you will adjust within time.

> Live life in your own comfortability.
>
> -Alexis Williams

CHAPTER 6

WHEN FINANCIAL AID HITS

My Experience

Let me tell you! I could not wait for financial aid to hit my account OKUURRYY. I was checking my bank account at midnight every time I knew it was going into my bank account! I bought my first car with my first financial aid check, yasss a car! I paid $800 for my lil hooptie and it got me from point A to point B! I also blew the rest of the money on clothes and food! Lots of food!

You might hear people say that you are going to gain the freshman fifteen your first year of college. This is true! I gained over fifteen pounds while attending college. Mostly because I was eating junk food and not enough home-cooked meals. There were lots of vending machines throughout campus, so when I got hungry, I would get chips or candy. There were also fast-food restaurants at the food court where I used to eat almost every single day.

I did not have any bills to pay besides my cell phone bill and gas for my vehicle, and I also never had over $500 entirely to myself. I did not know how to manage my money and unfortunately, my entire financial aid check was gone within a month. Yes! A month! Due to not knowing how to manage my money correctly.

Since I was a first-generation college student, I qualified for university grants and loans, and believe me, a 5,000-loan sounded good at the time of offering. I took out a loan EVERY SINGLE YEAR! Why? I honestly did not have a reason other than wanting more money in my pocket.

Considering the fact that I resided in the dorms, I did not receive much money from financial aid. Someone informed me that I had years to pay the money back, therefore, I was not worried about any accumulated debt. I thought I was balling!

Once I completed college, I was $34,000 in debt from taking out loans and being greedy. Although I bought a car, books, and necessities, I should have been smarter with my finances.

What I Wish Someone Told Me About When Financial Aid Hits

- Choose a financial aid packet that covers your tuition, fees, and living expenses. Most financial aid packets are just enough to cover your necessities.

- If you do not have to take out a loan, please do not! I completely understand that everyone's situation is different, and you might need to take out a loan because financial aid did not cover your full tuition, to better your financial situation, to help out your family, etc. Before you make this decision, be sure to weigh all your options.

- Ask staff at your campus financial aid office if there are any grants that are available to you, research how to get a scholarship, use your resources and ask around before you make the final decision to take out a loan.

- You CAN afford to attend college. There are many programs and resources that can financially help you pay for college and create a plan.

- College Loopholes, Get a Plan Not a Student Loan written by Dr. Marita Kinney, 2/2020. https://www.udemy.com/course/college-loopholes/. This website can help you with strategies on how to graduate debt-free, get a plan not a student loan, and so much more. Please check out this course that is available to all!

- If you end up taking out a loan, try your best to start paying back your loan as soon as you can afford to because the interest on your loan will increase. Remember, each loan you take out will go on your credit which means that you will be responsible for paying back the loan in FULL.

- Use your money wisely because you will only get financial aid a couple of times throughout the year!

- You must think of ways that will help you save money. If you receive $5,000 in financial aid in August and this $5,000 has to last you until January, how are you going to manage your money correctly? The best thing to do is to write down all the things that you need not want. If you need a car, look into purchasing a used car. Be sure to split your money into sections so that it can last longer.

- If possible, you should also save some of your money in case you have to pay for a class in the long run. During my senior year of college, I had to withdraw from my statistics class because I knew I was going to fail the class, and sometimes withdrawing from a class is better than getting a fail for grade point average reasons. I ended up having to pay $900 out of my own pocket to retake the class in the summertime AFTER I walked the stage due to running out of financial aid.

- Another important factor to take into consideration is always maintaining at LEAST a 2.0 grade point average. For reasons such as being put on academic probation where you will be on the verge of losing your financial aid, being kicked out school, dorms, sports, and anything else you might be involved in.

Take Away

Being offered a big chunk of money at once may seem like a good opportunity at the time of the offer. Remember to keep in mind that any amount you take out, you will have to pay it back. All money isn't good money!

> Be smart with your finances, buy what you NEED not what you WANT.
>
> **-Alexis Williams**

CHAPTER 7

PEER PRESSURE

Your peers will be throwing a party every weekend! Whether the party is in the dorms, in someone else's home, or the club, trust me, you will know about it. There will be something popping every weekend! This is the time in college that everyone looks forward to!

My Experience

College parties were some of the best parties that I attended! They were usually free and lasted all night long! There were kickbacks during the school week and different campus events. For instance, there was a party that my friends wanted me to attend.

Friends: "Come on! come with us! We only going for a little while you will have more than enough time to sleep and get to class in the am. Don't worry most professors don't even check attendance anyway you'll be good trust me."

Me: "Okay fine I'll go."

The next morning my alarm went off and I thought *damn I don't feel like getting up, I'll just miss class this one time and get the notes from someone the next time we have class.* I then missed that class that I would have been in if I did not attend the party.

What does peer pressure mean? Peer pressure is defined as "Influence from members of one's peer group." Granted, I was grown and could make decisions on my own but I have never been put in a situation where I needed to choose to party over class in high school! It was extremely difficult for me to keep my balance. Unfortunately, I had to learn the hard way by playing catch up with my schoolwork from any class that I missed. There were also times where I missed taking a test because I was too tired from the previous night out, to attend class. Most professors will not let you make up a test unless you have a good reason for having missed class such as a death in your family or being sick. A missed test significantly dropped my grade in a class, and there I was again playing catch up with making sure I aced every other test.

College also consists of completing group projects in some of your classes. I had to keep in mind that It would be very selfish of me to not give my all on my part of the project because I was out partying all night. I thought, *what about the other members in my group who put 100%*

effort? No one else should have to pick up my slack from poor decision making. Days where I knew that I had a project to complete or a midterm, I tried to stay home and study versus going out and partying.

What I Wish Someone Would Have Told Me About Peer Pressure

- You see college movies and know that some college students may party all night long and is in class the next morning with bloodshot eyes and a hangover because they pulled an all-nighter. Going to class with a hangover is the same as not going to class. Yes, you were physically in attendance but were you mentally there? Did you take any notes? Did you remember what the professor discussed? Probably not.

- One missed day won't hurt. Yes, that may be true, ONE missed class will not hurt you, but several missed classes will hurt your grade in the class. Missing class should only be for if you are sick, there's a family emergency, or you did not have a way to get to class for whatever reason. Most of your friends will not have the same classes as you and they may not truly care whether you attend class or you don't.

- You must get in the habit of telling people NO and not feeling guilty afterward. Your friends should understand why you are telling them no if your reasoning is due to having an early class, midterms, projects, papers, etc. If they do not understand then cut them loose.

- Let's not forget about drugs! Say no to drugs! You may be at a party and your peers may offer you drugs or pressure you to try a little bit of the drug. Please do not partake! Drugs can be very addictive and can lead you down the wrong path. Most individuals who attend college also have a part-time job. Some jobs conduct drug tests and if you test positive for any substance, you will risk being fired. Drugs can also damage your brain cells and can cause permanent damage. For example, Marijuana may cause heart attacks, high blood pressure, strokes, and may damage your lungs. Marijuana may also cause memory loss and confusion. So please remember to say no to drugs!

- If you are an individual who knows how to balance between partying and attending class on time and getting your work done, then go ahead and party! Have fun! Turn up! Again, it is all about balance!

- Many people may attend college for reasons other than their own such as to keep the family tradition going, and to follow in your parent's footsteps. Some parents may tell you, "I was a doctor so you are going to be a doctor too." But what if you don't want to be a doctor, or a lawyer, etc. Will you still have the same drive to complete school? Probably not. But how do you tell your parents that you don't want to follow the career path that THEY chose without them disowning you or not accepting your opinion? First, you would need to get into the mindset of not letting other people's opinions get in the way of what you want. You must know that everyone is going to have an opinion on what another person is doing or have done. Unfortunately, this is the way our society is set up. After you have mastered being unbothered by others' opinions, having the conversation with your parents will become easier. You must find your own career path. You have to want it so bad that nothing or no one will be able to stand in your way.

- Don't lose focus and stay on track.

Take Away

Always remember that you have your entire life to turn up and have fun. You can turn up as much as you want once you are done with school. I am not saying that you should not attend parties and have a good time with your friends, but make sure that you are being responsible in the process. You can literally lose yourself and focus by hanging with the wrong crowd and making irrational decisions.

> Never lose sight of why you made the decision to attend college.
> When things get tough remember your why.
>
> **-Alexis Williams**

CHAPTER 8

TUTORING, AND OFFICE HOURS

My Experience

One of the main classes that I had trouble with was math. I HATED math! I didn't understand it! I did not understand the majority of the formulas and I didn't understand why we needed to know anything other than simple math for counting your change from a purchase.

I remember attending various classes and leaving the class confused as to what the lecture was about. I could not go to my family for help because they did not know the answers. I was afraid to tell my professor that I did not understand the material after each class. I was afraid that my peers would see me asking my professor for help and think less of me. One person who I was not afraid to share my fears with was my counselor from the Educational Opportunity Program. I informed her that I was afraid that I was going to fail because I did not understand the material. She then informed me that I should attend tutoring for the subject that I was having trouble with. She reassured me that I am not the only one who is having trouble in my classes and that I should attend my professor's office hours because there may not be a tutoring class for every class that I take.

I had to ask myself how bad did I want this. Did I attend college to not obtain my degree because of classes that I was having trouble with? I think not! I then began attending tutoring and my professor's office hours for each class that I had trouble with weekly. I was surprised at how many other students were also attending tutoring and office hours. If I did not attend tutoring, I would NOT have graduated from college, PERIOD! I had to put my pride aside and reach out for help!

Reach Out For Help

Being frustrated and overwhelmed is something that a lot of college students go through so don't feel alone. There are numerous resources that will be available to you if you are feeling stressed and overwhelmed such as onsite campus counseling. There are onsite counselors that can help you through your stressful phase. I use the word phase because having a stressful class is only temporary. Once you pass a class, you will never have to take that class again.

Managing stress, pain, and anxiety is always going to be a working progress. Talk to your peers about what you're going through and look into support groups on campus. Remember that you are not alone.

What I Wished Someone Would Have Told Me About Tutoring And Office Hours

- There may come a time when you are drowning in class because you do not understand the material, or you have a professor that is not teaching the class right or you can't fully understand what your professor is saying. This is the time where you should ask questions and attend office hours and tutoring!

- Your midterms and papers will come quickly, and most of the time, they are all within the same week. It is important for you to make time to study for each class and attend your professor's office hours and or tutoring if you do not understand the material. The best thing that you can do is purchase a planner to write your important dates down.

- Making flashcards will also help you with remembering the material for each class. Studying can be very time-consuming so be sure to plan out the days you are going to study and be sure to stick to those days. If you study an hour or two each day, you will not have to cram all of the material into your brain a couple of days before your test. Don't work harder than you need to.

- Your professor will give you a syllabus for every class you take. The syllabus will have your professor's office hours. Usually, professors have office hours once or twice a week. Attending your professor's office hours gives you the opportunity to ask questions and get a better clarification on any question you may have. If your professor's office hours do not work with your schedule, you can ask your professor to meet with you a different day and time if their schedule permits it. If you are taking online classes, you can speak with your professor over the phone or via video chat. Your professors should know your name or remember your face. Not because you were that person in class asking a numerous amount of questions and did not let anyone else talk, but because you participated, got good grades, attend office hours, and was present.

- You can also start your own tutoring group with some of the individuals in your class. Again, don't be afraid to ask for help! Most of your peers might feel the same way you feel but are afraid to speak up. You can ask your peers if they do or don't understand the material, after that, you can ask if they would like to meet before class or after class to go over the material. Doing this will give you the motivation to know that you are not alone.

- Some individuals are afraid to ask for help. Some might think that they are too cool to attend office hours or a tutoring group. I was not one of those individuals. I needed to attend tutoring and office hours in order to pass various classes. The cool thing about tutoring and office hours is that they are two different things which means you can get double the help! Triple if you and your classmates start your own tutoring group for a specific class.

- Attending tutoring and office hours are extremely important in making sure you understand the material, passing the class, and developing relationships with your peers and your professors. Even if you understand the material, you should still attend your professor's office hours from time to time. You never know when you may need a letter of recommendation in the future!

Take Away

Tutoring and office hours are free and are offered daily! Don't be afraid to take advantage of the opportunity!

> Please don't be afraid to seek help.
>
> -Alexis Williams

CHAPTER 9

GET INVOLVED WITH YOUR CAMPUS!

At the beginning of every fall semester, there will be a welcome week, this is where you can mix and mingle with your peers to see what your campus is offering. Usually, students stop by the booths on their way to class or on their way home. The booths provide students with various information on different classes, job opportunities, health information and so much more!

My Experience

Due to being accepted to California State University Los Angeles conditionally through the Educational Opportunity Program, I had the opportunity to get to know staff, and attend events that they had. I stayed in the Educational Opportunity Program office because

I loved all the counselors and the advice they gave me. One day, the Educational Opportunity Program staff made an announcement stating that they were looking for four students to travel to Alabama for the Civil Rights Movement Tour. The requirements were writing an essay and attending an interview. I applied and got chosen with ALL expenses paid. This was my first time on a plane, and I was extremely excited to walk on history.

I was also chosen to speak at the Educational Opportunity Program workshops for students who were struggling in remedial math due to me finally passing my remedial math courses. I was always able to count on the staff from the Educational Opportunity Program.

During my junior year of college, I decided to get an on-campus job! Cal State LA had a place called the career center. The career center posted on-campus jobs that were vacant. I worked at the advisory department for Business and Economics for two years as the front desk receptionist. Working on campus was amazing because I worked around my school schedule. I went to class during the day and worked three to four hours after class. Because I was in school, I could only work part-time which was twenty hours per week.

Getting involved with my campus was also a good way for me to get to know my peers and the different staff!

What I Wish Someone Told Me About Getting Involved With Campus

- Look into the career center on your campus to find out about jobs are open!

- Look into taking extracurricular activities! Do you like to dance? Do you sing? Do you play basketball? Are you interested in community involvement? Do you draw, etc.? Whatever it is that you are interested in, your campus should have a course or something similar, available for you to enroll in. Participating in an extracurricular activity weekly will also keep you motivated in attending class.

- Look into joining a fraternity or a sorority! Brotherhood and Sisterhood are good to have while attending college as extra motivation because you will have to maintain a certain grade point average to stay a part of the fraternity or sorority. Joining a sorority or fraternity can help you create lifelong friendships, build connections, attend more social activities and so much more! Joining a sorority or fraternity can be important in making connections while in school and after graduating college because you will forever have that sisterhood or brotherhood.

Take away

Having peers and staff to go to when you are feeling overwhelmed is especially important, but if you are not involved with your campus then how would you have that opportunity? Try your best to become involved with your campus by joining clubs, organizations, and looking into what your campus has to offer. This will also alleviate stress because you will be participating in something that you are interested in.

> It never hurts to try something new,
> after all you can stop going at anytime.
>
> -Alexis Williams

CHAPTER 10

LIFE GOT IN THE WAY

What I Wish Someone Told YOU About Life Getting In Your Way

- Were you working a part-time job, was doing extremely well, and they offered you a full-time position? You took it because the money was good, and you were financially struggling? You can still attend college part-time while you work. You can also take online classes!

- Were you attending college and was not receiving any support from your friends or family? College can be draining, stressful, overwhelming, and could cause you to have a lot of anxiety. Sometimes your family and friends may not completely understand the stressors you are going through while attending college. There is a therapist on campus that you can speak with. Most individuals are afraid to speak to a therapist because they may feel embarrassed, judged, afraid to open up, etc. You can join a peer support group, that way you will have the opportunity to listen to your peers going through similar situations. You can also speak to your academic counselor! I met with my academic counselor every couple of months to make sure that I was on track to graduate. There were times when I informed my academic counselor of the stressors that I was going through, and they gave me words of encouragement and motivation.

- Were you attending college and had a death of a family member or friend which caused you to go into depression and slacked with your work? Again, we are human, and life happens. Dealing with the death of any loved one is difficult. You can take an academic leave from college while you are grieving and return when you are in a better mental space.

- Were you attending college and had a child? Having a child is always a blessing! You can take an academic leave from college while you are tending to your child. Sometimes parents may not have a babysitter while continuing school. Some colleges offer childcare on campus. One of the main requirements is having a certain number of units in order to qualify. You can also take online classes in the comfort of your own home! Some individuals may not like taking online classes for various reasons but remember that this is an option.

- No money to buy a computer? Everyone's situation is different. Some people cannot save any money and are living paycheck to paycheck, if you can save $10 from each paycheck, to go towards a computer within a year, you will have enough income to purchase a laptop. You can also contact your campus to see if they have any programs that may help with obtaining a laptop.

- Don't have any Wi-Fi at home? You can walk to the nearest place that does such as Starbucks, the library, a bookstore, or hotspot on your cellular device, and so on. You can sit in one of these places while completing your work.

- Did your car break down while you were driving to and from campus? Don't have a car at all? Don't know how to drive? Got tired of catching the bus every day? Financial aid can help you pay for a car. If you do not qualify for financial aid, you can possibly take out a loan, create a go fund me account, or get a part-time job so that you can save your money to purchase a car. You can also carpool to school with your peers! Don't be afraid to ask for help!

- Do you feel like you are too old to go back to school? Did you start school and could not finish because life got in the way and now it has been years later, and you are thinking about going back but are afraid that you are too old? If you are currently 27, by the time you finish school you might be 31. Regardless if you start school or not, you'll still be 31 in four years so why not go for it? Remember, it is never too late to go back or start school! School does not have an age limit! Granted, you may be a little older than most individuals who are in some of your classes due to the fact that most individuals attend college right out of high school, but so what! You should not care about what anyone else thinks!

- Continue to say positive affirmations to yourself such as "I can do this," "I am not too old," "I am capable," "I am deserving," "I am ready," "I am strong," and "I can do anything I put my mind to."

Take Away

We are all human and life happens! Regardless of what situation you are in, there is ALWAYS another alternative! It may not be the one that you want but remember your WHY. Somethings that you want to do take a lot of self-discipline and dedication. Remember that the situation you are in is only temporary and you too will get through it. When you are in tough situations, you have to look at the good even if you feel like there aren't any. There will always be good in any situation and a way to make things happen. Remember that if there is a will there is always a way. If plan A does not work don't get discouraged, create plan B.

> Despite fear, finish the job

-Kobe Bryant, (Rest in Heaven)

CHAPTER 11

IS COLLEGE FOR ME?

Activity

College is **NOT** for everyone and that is perfectly okay. But if college is not for you, what is for you? Do you know what your purpose is? If so, do you know the steps that you need to take to get there? If not, do you know how to find your purpose?

Directions:

Write down as many things you can think of that you like to do, things that excite you, your talents, abilities, and positions you can see yourself in.

_____
_____
_____

Now, look at the list you just wrote down and ask yourself what it will take for your to get to where you want to be.

Finding your purpose, drive, and vision

Based on what you would like to pursue, you may not need to obtain a bachelor's degree to be successful. You can attend a trade school, obtain certificates and other degrees that take less time to complete such as:

- Real estate agent
- Hairstylist
- Business owner
- Chef
- Web Developer
- Makeup artist
- Singer/ rapper
- Actor
- Piolet

And so many more!

Additionally, if you attended a community college and only earned an associate's degree, there are also jobs that require JUST an associate's degree and or college credits such as:

- Registered nurse
- Paralegal
- Dental Hygienist

And so many more!

Many people have become millionaires by researching what it is that they wanted to do, how to do it, and presented it to the world through various forms such as social media, attending events, and being a part of their communities.

If you are not going to obtain a degree, you might have to work extra hard to get where you want to be. This will also require sleepless nights, running into walls, doors after doors, and being knocked down. Remember to get back up. One thing that I have learned throughout my journey is that not everyone is going to be happy for you. Therefore, you should not share your dreams with everyone because people pray on your downfall or make negative comments on YOUR goals and you do not need that type of negativity in your life. Share your dreams and vision with individuals who fully support you, who are not jealous of your success, and who genuinely believe and supports your dreams.

However, some job positions may require you to have your degree such as:

- Social workers
- Lawyers

- Teachers
- Some doctors

And so many more! So, if you realize that you will need to obtain a degree for your career path, start now!

Take away

Start googling and researching the occupation you want to pursue and the steps needed to get there. Anything is possible so long as you put effort into what you're striving for. Don't become content with where you are now, start creating a better life for yourself.

Manifest the life YOU want!

> We tend to look at others around us who have fancy cars, nice homes, careers, money, etc. and at times, we may become sad, lost, and eager, because we are socially constructed by social media to believe that everyone should live a certain lifestyle. However, each lifestyle someone else lives, is for them and their own comfortability. You have to find your own path, journey and comfortability.
>
> **-Alexis Williams**

CHAPTER 12

THE FINISH LINE

My finish line

I began attending college in 2011, I did not earn my degree until 2017 which means that it took me six years to graduate college. Some people graduate in four years, some in seven years. Time means absolutely nothing. The most important thing was that I received my degree no matter how much time it took me. I was the one putting in the work, not anyone else. College took a lot of time, hard work, and dedication, but nothing was more rewarding than sticking through something that I worked so hard for.

After graduating from college, I was working as a behavioral interventionist which consisted of working with children in their homes and at schools on correcting their behaviors such as tantrums, outbursts, speech, etc. I started to become very content with the way my life was going that I did not feel the need to look for another source of income because I was making decent money. Here it is, I have my own place, a car, traveling, I was doing the damn thang all by myself. I thought to myself, *I'm stable, I'm good, life could not get any better than this.* WRONG! Never and I mean NEVER should I have settled for anything less than what my degree permitted. I should have never settled for anything less than the pay rate I deserved with having my degree. I spent hours studying, crying, sleepless nights, losing friends, developing anxiety, being uncomfortable, and so much more just to settle for the first job I got after college that was NOT in my career path. Hell no! After this realization, I started applying for jobs in my career field. A year and a half later, I got my dream job! It took time, but it was worth the wait.

What I Wish Someone Told YOU About The Finish Line

- Many people may come from families that have not succeeded or accomplished anything. Breaking generational curses has always been one of my goals. Just because you have not seen it done, does not mean that it cannot be done. We all have the same 24 hours in a day to work on goals.

- Some individuals take years to figure out their purpose, some still do not know what their purpose is and that is okay. You are on your own time and in your own lane.
- When you find out what it is that inspires, motivates, and feeds your soul, you will start to feel like you are on the right path in your life.
- Results may not happen right away or when you want them to happen. Many people graduate from college and it may take them over a year to find a job in their career field, and many people still have not found a job. If you are applying yourself every single day, you WILL succeed.
- After receiving your bachelor's degree, some individuals continue onto receiving their master's degree and or doctoral degree. The more degrees you have, the more experience you will have, and the more income you will have as well! If I had a master's degree for the job I currently have, my pay rate would be higher than what it currently is.
- Did you know that you can obtain your PhD without obtaining your master's degree in SOME professions? 2020 The PhD Project, https://www.phdproject.org/ has collaborated with a numerous amount of Universities that can help you with obtaining a PhD degree. Please check out the above website.

- After you receive your degree, your pay rate should be higher than an individual who only has a high school diploma. Therefore, finding your purpose, drive, and vision is extremely important because it will lead you to know where you will need to start. Obtaining your degree is something that NO ONE can take away from you. This is something that you earned and will have for the rest of your life. Be proud!

- If you have decided that college is not for you, make sure that you are working extra hard to receive enough income to live comfortably. Some entrepreneurs such as hairstylists, artist, actors, etc. are making more than individuals who have their degrees and this is because they worked hard to get to where they are today, and they love what they do. If you love what you do, work will not feel like work.

- After you figure out your purpose, drive, and vision, you may want to start another project. Don't limit yourself to one job. Many people have different talents. You may be a teacher because you love children and feeding their souls, but you also may love to cook and want to have your own restaurant someday. Why not do both? You can work on your other dreams after you are finished with work. Although you are at your finish line with your main occupation, you can always start another race.

Take away

You may not always get your dream job right after you graduate college. Some people do and that is amazing if you do, but in reality, things take time. Continue to apply yourself, have patience, and remember that everyone's finish line is different.

> Picture yourself with your dream job, car, business, home, money, anything you want to imagine. Place yourself there, feels amazing right? Open your eyes, write down the steps you need to take for you to get there. Work on it every single day. With time, your vision will be your reality.
>
> **-Alexis Williams**

> "The Marathon Continues"
>
> - Nipsey Hustle (Rest in Peace)

Self-Care

It is important to maintain self-care while navigating through college. You might experience various obstacles that may make you want to give up on school. Developing self-care strategies can help reduce stress, keep you healthy, balanced, motivated, and so much more.

Activity

Self-care comes in many different forms such as physical, emotional, social, spiritual, etc. What does self-care look like for you?

_____
_____
_____
_____
_____
_____
_____
_____
_____
_____
_____

Take away

Be sure to take care of yourself! Self-care can improve your mental, emotional, and physical health. Try to practice self-care weekly.

> You CAN and you WILL!
> Believe in yourself!
>
> -Alexis Williams

GRADUATION

Graduation is one of the best times of the year for college students. This is the time where you get to purchase your cap and gown and try it on a bunch of times while looking in the mirror *like I really did it!* This is the time where your family and friends celebrate YOU. Graduating college is an accomplishment that you will forever be proud of.

Most colleges may have multiple graduation ceremonies such as a general graduation ceremony with your entire school, and or a cultural graduation in which you can participate in both or neither. Weeks before graduation, I decided to participate in black grad. Black grad was any individual who identified themselves as being African American. Staff informed me that they are looking for two speakers for the graduation and the topic was: what does it mean to be a black graduate today. I was so excited to submit my essay! I loved writing and I knew that I would make my friends and family proud if I was chosen to represent my community! I submitted my essay and did not hear anything back from the staff. I thought, *welp I tried*! Maybe they picked someone else. A couple of weeks later, I went to the office to pick up my tickets for the graduation ceremony. I then gave the staff my name and my student ID. A staff member then stated, "Your Alexis!? It's nice to meet you, you will be sitting in the front row at the graduation ceremony." I was so confused, I thought they had me mixed up with someone else.

I responded, "Why?"

The staff member responded, "Your essay was chosen; you will be one of our speakers. No one contacted you?"

My heart literally dropped. I began to get extremely excited! I then stated, "No one has contacted me, but thank you so much!" The next couple of days I read my essay repeatedly so that I could memorize it. The staff member informed me that my essay would be available for me to look at as I stood on the stage, but I wanted to memorize it to the best of my ability. I kept thinking that I was not going to be able to memorize this essay. *What was I thinking submitting an essay anyway! I can't speak in front of people, what if I start stuttering? What if I get stage fright?* All of these things were going through my mind! I then told myself that *I CAN do this, and I WILL do this!* And there I was speaking at my graduation in front of hundreds of people! I was nervous, excited, and proud of myself.

What does it mean to be a Black Graduate Today?

*College has always been my dream. I remember praying to get into Cal State LA as I will be the first in my family to graduate from college as many of you may also be. Being an African American female from South Los Angeles, statistically, I was not supposed to get into college let along graduate. Statistics suggest that I was not going to succeed, that I was either going to drop out of school or work a minimum wage job for the rest of my life, but I **REFUSE** to be another statistic. This system was never designed for us. It was built by us but never designed to shelter us. African Americans have undergone a tremendous amount of discrimination, especially when it came to obtaining a good education. Being a black graduate today means that we are making our ancestors proud and proving to our society that we are extremely stronger than a system that was not designed to see blacks succeed.*

Being a black graduate today means that we are working beyond our expectations and limitations. Black excellence is Dr. Martin Luther King, Barack Obama, Rosa Parks, (the list goes on) and now all of us sitting here today is a part of that history. This is what the media would never portray. We must remember how we got here, African Americans have faced the hardships of racism and segregation within the United States and all around the world. The Black Lives Matter Movement is more than just a hashtag there have been battles, protests, and riots in an attempt to end racism and create equal opportunity in the black community. Though there has been an end to slavery and African Americans have gained the rights through various movements, we are still being denied our natural-born rights every day through the use of racism.

Being a black college graduate is seen as a threat to today's society. America knows that our culture is a threat! Why do you think they chose our race to be slaves? Because an educated man is a free man. Many people say that the American Dream is based on a person's point of view and their own personal goals in life, but how can the American Dream be achieved if not every human being has the same equal opportunities as the person standing next to them? Until there is an end to racism, and everyone is viewed as equals, the American Dream will never truly exist. Everyone sitting in this room has strived to make their dream a reality and we are one step further in reaching our full potential. As a black graduate today and as a woman, it is empowering to see how far we've come to get here. We live in a society where the black culture is underrepresented, and I am extremely proud to stand here today and say I made it!

– Alexis Williams
2017 black Graduation Speech

> Someone can take away your car if you don't pay your car note, someone can evict you from your apartment if you don't pay your rent, you can get fired from your job if you are not performing well, But NO ONE can take away YOUR degree because this is something YOU earned and will have for the rest of your life. PERIOD!
>
> **-Alexis Williams**

Create Your Vision Board

At the beginning of the book I asked you to write down 10 goals that you would like to accomplish within the next five years. I want you to now project them onto a vision board. If you do not know what a vision board looks like, you can look at the cover of this book and or google vision board samples. It does not have to be a fancy vision board with lots of expensive material. You can print pictures, go to the dollar store to get the board, and whatever else you would like your board to reflect. You will then tape or glue the objects that you want onto your vision board.

When you are done, place your vision board in a place where you will have no choice but to look at it every single day. Creating a vision board will continue to keep you motivated in accomplishing your goals.

> Nothing that you do will be easy. If it was, then we would all be doing something else, remember to plan, strive, and achieve.
>
> **-Alexis Williams**

> I hope after reading this book, you push yourself to become the greatest you.
>
> -Alexis Williams

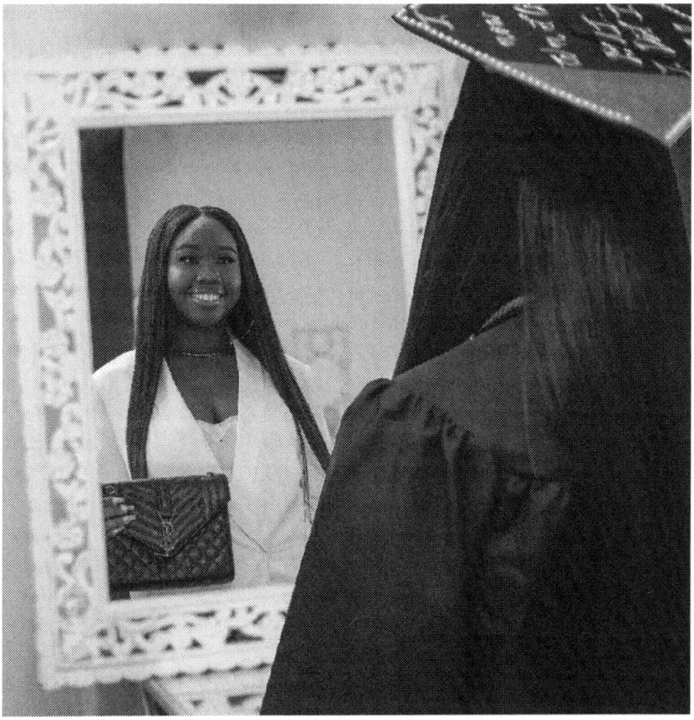

About Author

Alexis Williams was born and raised in various locations in Los Angeles, California. She was raised in a single-parent household and is the youngest child. Alexis Williams is the first in her family to graduate college. She received her bachelor's degree in Sociology from California State University Los Angeles and is currently working at her dream job. Alexis is well known for being goal-driven, staying focused, and being open-minded. Her compassion, willingness to help others, and her transparency has helped her become who she is today. Alexis's goal is to become a mentor to individuals about the difficulties in completing college and overcoming fears.

PTP
Pure Thoughts Publishing LLC

Made in the USA
Las Vegas, NV
02 November 2020

10504760R00069